Erika the Dummy Fairy
& the magic dummy
By Andrea Locket

Baby Sammy has arrived

Baby Sammy had just arrived
The Frog Prince was soon at her side
He needed to tell Erika to drop by
With a magical dummy so the baby
won't cry

The Frog Prince finds Erika
the Dummy Fairy

The Frog Prince finds Erika in Fairyland
He tells her to wave her magical hand
Prepare a dummy for new baby Sammy
So she will never become unhappy

Erika casts a magic spell

Erika waves her magic wand around
There are sparkles, stars and a popping
sound
All of a sudden a magical dummy pops up
To make sure baby Sammy has the best of
luck

The Frog Prince takes the
Dummy to baby Sammy

The Frog Prince is happy now as well
Sammy is protected by Erika's magic spell
It will last until she's grown tall
When she'll no longer need a dummy at all

He tells Sammy that the magic is on loan
It'll help her sleep and stop her feeling alone
The magic contained in Erika's fairy spell
Will keep her safe, snug, happy and well

Sammy sleeps soundly with
her magical dummy

The spell lasts until Sammy is all grown
Then Erika visits when she is all alone
I am so pleased you have slept happily each
night
It's time to give the magic back and do
what's right

Erika tells Sammy that she
only has to give up her dummy
when she's ready. And not to
worry.

I don't want you to be unhappy and glum Erika says
When the Frog Prince comes to visit one day
He'll only come when your dummy has been outgrown
And you don't need it to stop you feeling sad and alone

The Frog Prince is so proud of Sammy for giving up her dummy, and he gives her a gift.

Sammy is happy to give up her dummy today
Another baby needs the magic so she gave it away
The Frog Prince is so proud he has a gift from the fairies
For sharing the magic with the other babies

Baby Jessica has arrived and
the Frog Prince gives her
Sammy's Dummy

The Frog Prince is so proud of Sammy for giving up her dummy, and he gives her a gift.

If you are ready to give up your dummy one day
Leave it under your bed and listen to what the Frog Prince has to say
I'm so pleased you have slept happy each night
It's time to give the magic back and do what's right

The Frog Prince bringing a
gift from fairyland

Sleep tight and the fairies will send you magical dreams

The End

Printed in Great Britain
by Amazon

27761067R10016